GLORY

GLO

ORY

PHOTOGRAPHS OF ATHLETES
RICHARD CORMAN

WILLIAM MORROW AND COMPANY, INC.

NEW YORK

For Patricia and William

For my father,
who will always be my
greatest champion
because he lives his life
with compassion,
humility, and dignity.
This book reflects
what he has inspired me to
see and feel.

FOREWORD
KEN BURNS

WE LOOK AT PHOTOGRAPHY WITH AN UNARTICULATED EXPECTATION OF TRUTH, FACT. RARELY DO WE ASK it to do more. When it does, we are stirred—awakened and galvanized into a new relationship with ourselves and given a new perception of the world around us. When it does, we are also pushed closer to an understanding of the complicated concentration of skin and muscles, thought and heart, intention and limitation, that we call human beings.

Richard Corman's magnificent photographs recall in nearly every moment and gesture the possibilities of an artistic vision dedicated to the highest aspirations of human endeavor. His work is subversive in the best sense of the word; these images are revealing, brutally honest, unflinchingly direct. And they record in big moments and small, among the famous and the ordinary, the gifted and the challenged, larger truths relevant to all of us. As these images accrue and resonate in our memories, this beautiful book takes on the character of an esoteric encyclopedia, cataloging and enumerating the many ways we mere mortals achieve a kind of grace normally reserved for the gods. That Corman has done this with photographs of sport makes his achievement all the more remarkable.

Sport is our tribal worship; it is ancient necessity, survival of the fittest, ritualized and brought to the center of our modern life. In our sports, we find a mesmerizing intersection of fact and myth. The fact part is simple: who won, in what time, how far, what weight, how many points. But sport is also a kind of theater of hope and dreams, like the Japanese Noh drama, wherein we play out in the gritty, sweaty efforts of others, both like us and not like us, the subtlest and most complicated facets of our individual and collective desires. Though they are utterly nonessential as human activity goes, the games we play paradoxically reveal our essence and we place in those games the expectation that something larger, more mysterious, more transforming might arise in our ordinary lives.

Corman's photographs are truly GLORYous. From the accomplished professionals like Ken Griffey, Jr., and Jackie Joyner-Kersee and Michael Jordan to the anonymous amateurs, from children with a lifetime of hope ahead to the heartbreakingly pure angels who compete in the Special Olympics, his eye ennobles sport, levels it, equalizes it, makes it his—and ours.

His pictures suggest a majesty beyond our day-to-day existence. They show exquisite human machines at the peak of their powers, new bodies as yet untested but pregnant with future challenge, and older athletes radiating with the residue of past effort, past glory. They show black skin and white skin, new skin and wrinkled skin. They show muscles in tension and in repose. They show bodies of every kind, perfect and flawed, conscious and self-conscious, full and spent. They show the undeniable fact of loss and victory, that is to say, the commonplaces of everyday life—but here, in this book, it is elevated, transcendent, magical.

Here sport is movement, art, dance, ballet. Here the best kind of eroticism is on display, depleted of lust and voyeurism, replaced with wonder, intimacy, love. Here are pictures of athletes from around the world, all pursuing different sports: men, women, old, young, yet within Corman's generous sights, each pursues his or her goal with the same kind of palpable hunger. That striving, that hunger is at the heart of who we humans are. Without it, we shrink from view; with it, we are merely candidates for inclusion in this great work of insight.

INTRODUCTION
RICHARD CORMAN

AS A CHILD I LOOKED UP TO THEM. AS A TEENAG-ER I WAS IN AWE. AS A YOUNG MAN THEY WERE my heroes. Whether playing touch football with my dad in Riverside Park in New York City or watching Willis Reed limp onto the floor at Madison Square Garden in the seventh game of the 1969 NBA championships, I was filled with the desire to be like the athletes I admired. I played with a fervor so profound that it became tangible: It felt like something that could be touched and held onto. I now know why: That intensity brought a dignity.

As a photographer, I am still drawn to that dignity. From it grows a self-respect that is rooted not so much in extraordinary skill as in the balance between pride and humility, between confidence and vulnerability. When we allow ourselves to become vulnerable, to take chances, and to risk our pride, that is it when we find our own glory.

My heroes today range from the Special Olympians, who claim victory even when the scoreboard might show otherwise because they compete with warmth; to the BMX bikers whom I admire for their fearlessness; to the world champions, such as Jackie Joyner-Kersee, who are fueled by passion; to Muhammad Ali, a man of genius and honesty. When the outside world fades away and great athletes, famous and obscure, professional and amateur, are alone with only their bodies and their sport, they are left with the rawness of their own athleticism, their own drive, and their own victory.

Sport at its best, at its most human, is able to inspire an innocence and joy that is unique to each of us.

ITALIAN BOY, 1984

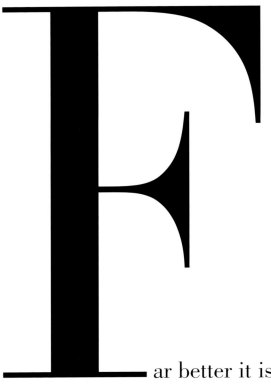Far better it is to dare

mighty things, to win glorious triumphs,

even though checkered by failure,

than to take rank with those

poor spirits who neither enjoy nor

suffer too much, because they

live in the gray twilight that knows

not victory nor defeat.

THEODORE ROOSEVELT

GLORY

PETER BOAL, 1995

The glory
of sport comes from dedication,
determination, and desire.
Achieving success and personal
glory in athletics
has less to do with wins and
losses than it does with
learning how to prepare yourself,
so that at the end of
the day, whether on the track or in
the office, you know
that there was nothing more you
could have done to reach your
ultimate goal.

———————

JACKIE JOYNER-KERSEE

JACKIE JOYNER-KERSEE, 1996

FELIX "TITO" TRINIDAD, 1998

SHARON MONPLAISIR, 1992

GAIL DEVERS, 1992

LANCE ARMSTRONG, 1996

ALLEN JOHNSON, 1996

Sport is quite a simple thing. It is play, and in play, people of all ages find the chance to engage their most profound emotions—love, fear, excitement, disappointment, anger, and joy. But in sport as in play, the rules and the terrain make it all straightforward: kick the ball, go the distance, give your best. In the comfort of the game, we can enjoy the profound.

The mix of profundity and play is potent. Everyone reaches for more in life, and everyone hopes that his or her personal adventure might actually mean something to the world. The glory of sport is born at the moment when the game and the person become one, when all the complexity of one's life finds a moment to emerge in the game.

So it is no surprise that the Special Olympics athlete has an exceptional ability to create the glory of sport. For him or her, the world rarely watches, rarely cheers, rarely cares. But on the playing field, a chance is given and the chance is taken with courage. So the smiles at Special Olympics are more present, the cheers roar louder, the hopes have more power, and the thrills are more shared. But most important, at Special Olympics, sheer simplicity wins the day. It is found in the eyes and hands and face of the athlete who, despite every obstacle, stands before the world to say, "I count, and I, too, can do something good."

That is the glory of sport.

TIMOTHY SHRIVER, Ph.D.

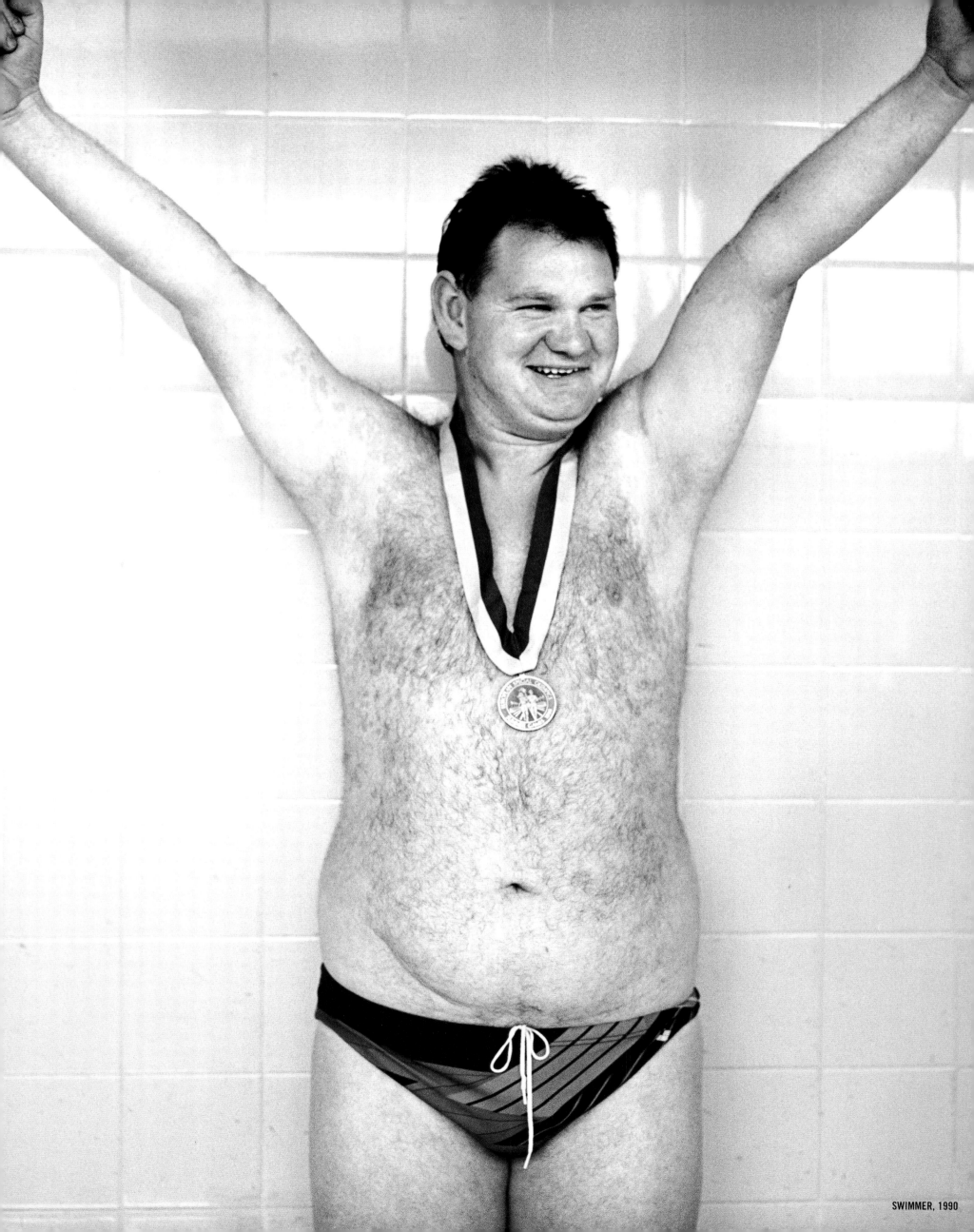

SWIMMER, 1990

MICHAEL JORDAN, 1991

George Patton once said that the greatest pursuit in life is glory—more than fame, more than fortune—because glory is so fleeting, so short-lived. He's right. A person can live a lifetime marked by fame and fortune. Glory exists solely within a moment, and that's why it is so pursued and so elusive. Glory is also inextricably tied to two other life pursuits—happiness and success. Happiness is knowing what you want. Success is getting what you want. But glory is the ultimate experience of wanting and enjoying what you finally have.

ROY FIRESTONE

KEITH VAN HORN, 1998

DARCI KISTLER, 1995

Few in the world are neutral, or on the fence, about sport. Sport inspires passionate feelings of either devotion or disgust. Is it beautiful or ugly? Good or evil? Civilizing or brutalizing? The tug of war has raged. Only recently, a new model has emerged with sport seen, at its essence, as ultimate paradox. How else can one explain how in sport men reveal their emotions while women experience their strength and assertiveness? Children learn life lessons and adults re-create the play of childhood. Executives relax and the bored become exhilarated. For the overweight participant, sport is part of a regimen for reducing; the underweight participates to build and define.

Cheating runs rampant and gallant self-sacrifice is ordinary.

Sport, indeed, is a bare canvas to which we present our *selves* . . . fully, completely, and exquisitely.

———————————

DR. CAROLE A. OGLESBY

BONNIE BLAIR, 1998

BASKETBALL CAMP, 1995

ANDRES ESPINOSA, 1994

Playing 2,131
consecutive ball games and breaking
Lou Gehrig's record had
nothing to do with extraordinary
talent, which I don't have, or a bionic body,
which I don't have either,
or a burning desire for the spotlight, which
can be really fun at times
and is really gratifying, but has its drawbacks
as well. No, when I look back
over those fourteen seasons of consecutive
games with the Baltimore Orioles,
I have to agree with my
brother Bill's blunt conclusion. He says I
broke that record because
I could. The streak was an approach to the game.
I tried not to think about the
record at all. I just ducked my head
and met the challenges
of each day. One day at a time.

CAL RIPKEN, JR.

JOHN STARKS, 1993

I believe everything happens for a reason. I always try to remember how bad it could have been. I'm beating the odds. I could be in a wheelchair now. Or a grave. My God, it was so close.

_____

REGGIE BROWN

REGGIE BROWN, 1998

EDWIN MOSES, 1988

DANNY DROMGOOL, 1995

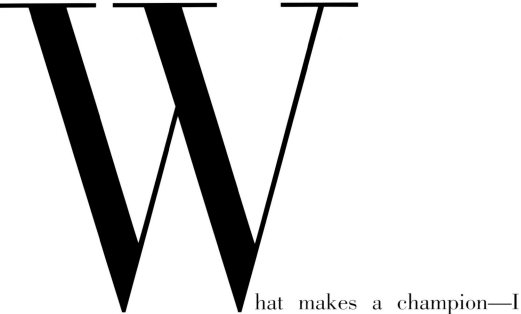

What makes a champion—I mean the legends, the top percentile who consistently dominate their opponents, perform at their highest level at the most crucial times, and ultimately distance themselves from the near-greats and the also-rans?

The champion's true edge exists solely in the mind. He has a profound sense of dissatisfaction with his accomplishments. Success and victory spur greater ambition; athletes perform at their best when the stakes are the greatest. In the champion's mind, he is never ahead. He distorts reality to serve his competitive purpose. He is always coming from behind, even when the score indicates he is destroying his opponent. He never believes he is performing as well as he actually is.

———————————

MARK MCCORMACK

MICHAEL JOHNSON, 1996

VICTOR BATTLE, 1997

Sport is the most powerful motivator in the world. I remember how my brother used to race against me when I was a little girl and make fun of me when he won. One day I decided I wasn't going to lose anymore. So I practiced on my own until I knew I was ready to face him again. I beat him that next race, and he never raced me again. I was inspired by the competition, and eager to see how far I could push myself.

That motivation was also one of the major factors in my rehabilitation from Graves' disease. I went through extensive thyroid radiation treatment. I kept pushing myself to heal. I would not give up. Sports had taught me never to quit. Beating the disease was an athletic challenge—but I was playing for my life.

GAIL DEVERS

GAIL DEVERS, 1992

JACKIE JOYNER-KERSEE, 1992

BRAD HUNT, 1998

AIMEE MULLINS, 1998

T

he word "athlete" needs no qualifiers. It matters not whether someone is professional or amateur, able-bodied or disabled, male or female. The power of the human will to compete and the drive to excel beyond the body's normal capabilities is most beautifully demonstrated in the arena of sport. Being an athlete allows one to break down the barriers of race, ethnicity, religion, gender, and poverty. An athlete experiences the emotions of pain and elation through triumph and defeat, through teamwork and individuality, as nothing more than a human being . . . that is the true glory of sport.

AIMEE MULLINS

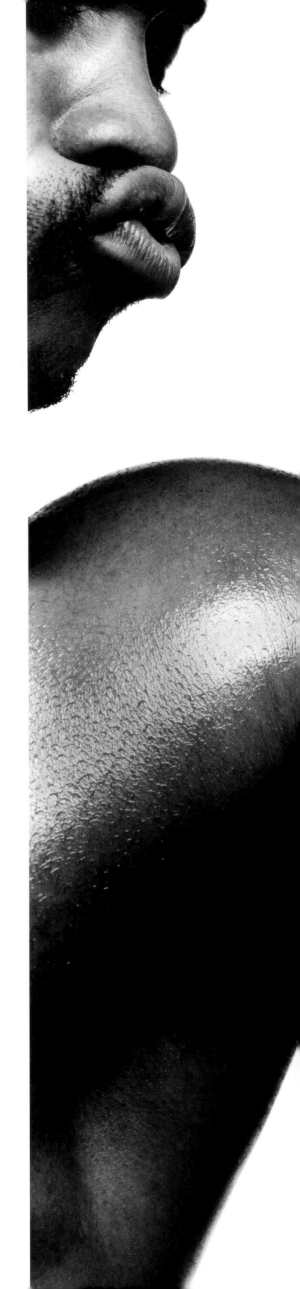

In *Raging Bull*, boxing becomes a searing landscape of a man's personal life, a life branded by power and violence, where battles are fought out of anger and victory, a matter of life and death. On film and in the ring, the power of sport is its ability to bring humanity back to certain basics—competition and survival.

ROBERT DE NIRO

ROY JONES, JR., 1995

TONY TUCKER, 1989

KIM BATTEN, 1996

MAYA LABAT AND L. B. TEJADA, 1996

RICKEY JACKSON, 1991

For that
one moment of glory,
whether winning
a Super Bowl or the
jubilation of
victory in any particular
event, all one
needs is a full-time
commitment of
dedication and effort.
To feel glory, you
must have passion for
what you want to
accomplish. Pure glory
can be achieved
by anyone. Glory can be
addictive. Once
felt, it can never last long
enough, but it is
also never forgotten.

JERRY RICE

HARRY CARSON, 1988

NANCY KERRIGAN, 1992

RUNNER, 1991

S

ports
can unite a group of
people from different
backgrounds, all working
together to achieve a
common goal. And even if
they fall short, sharing
that journey is an
experience they'll never
forget. It can teach some
of the most fundamental
and important human values:
dedication, perseverance,
hard work, and teamwork.
It also teaches us how
to handle our success and
cope with our failure.
So, perhaps the greatest glory
of sport is that it teaches
us so much about life itself.

AHMAD RASHAD

MARK O'MEARA AND TIGER WOODS, 1998

LUKE WILSON AND OWEN WILSON, 1983

NEW YORK YANKEES, 1998

G

reat players are not dependent on the adulation of others. They give rather than take. Even in the midst of defeat or failure, they look inward to see what they could have done differently to have prevented a loss or an error. They never blame someone else on their team or look for excuses. Great players separate their performance from their self-worth, and thus are capable of objectively analyzing their deficiencies, supporting others, and encouraging their teammates.

DONNA A. LOPIANO, Ph.D.

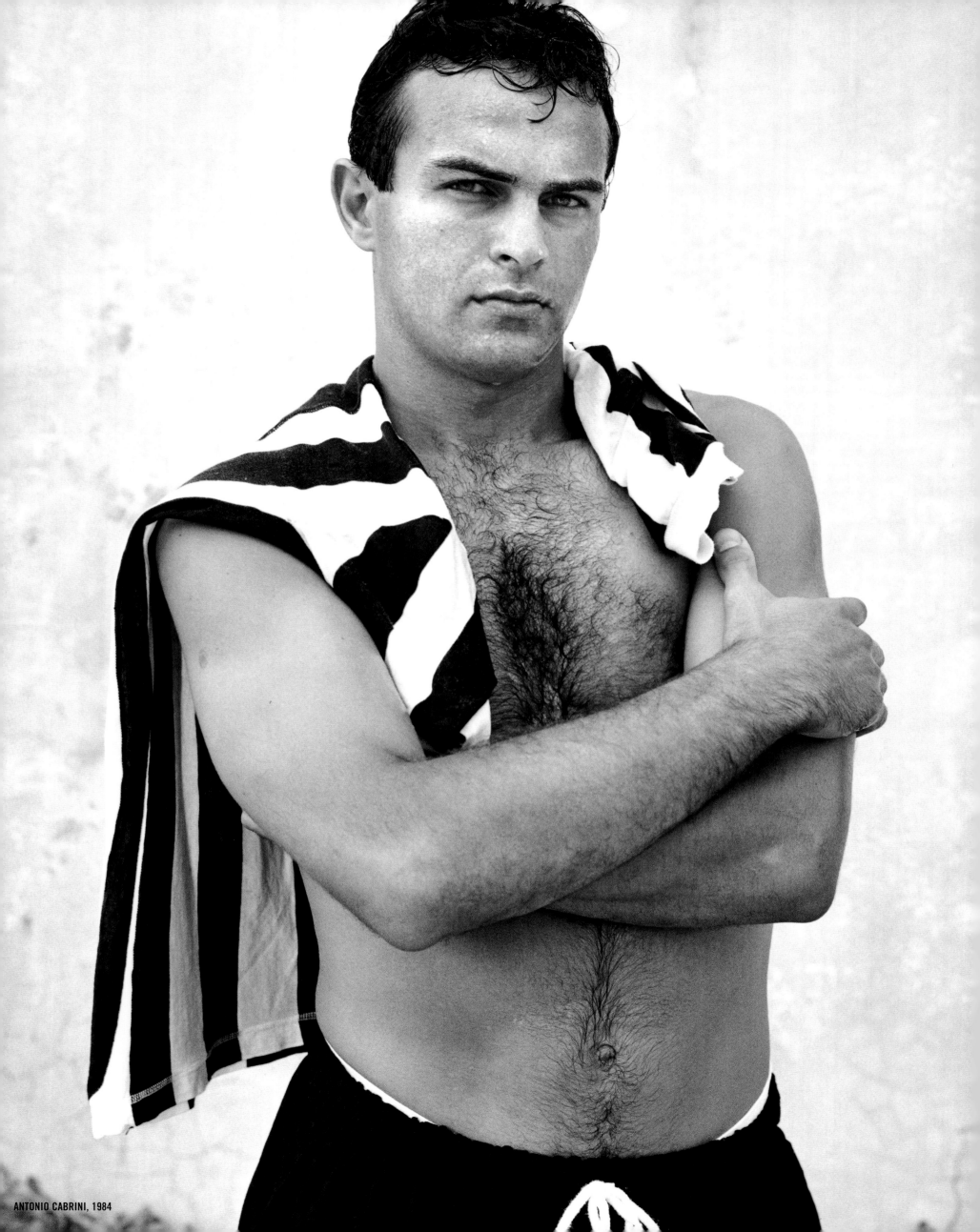

ANTONIO CABRINI, 1984

JULIE KENT, 1992

CONNIE PRICE-SMITH, 1988

few days before the 1964 Tokyo Olympic Games, discus thrower Al Oerter tore cartilage in his rib cage during a practice session. Breathing was painful; competing seemed impossible. "You die before you don't make an attempt at the Olympic Games," said Oerter. Trailing, Oerter made one all-out attempt on his next-to-last throw. When he released the discus, he temporarily blacked out. Quickly, he revived to hear the announcement that he had just set a new Olympic record that would give him the gold medal.

Four years later, in Mexico City, John Stephen Akhwari of Tanzania ran the Olympic marathon. Bloodied and bandaged after suffering an injury during the race, Akhwari was the last man to finish, more than an hour after the winner was crowned. Akhwari simply said, "My country did not send me to the Olympic Games to start the race, they sent me to finish the race." I have often debated with myself whether it was Al Oerter or John Stephen Akhwari who gained the greater glory.

BUD GREENSPAN

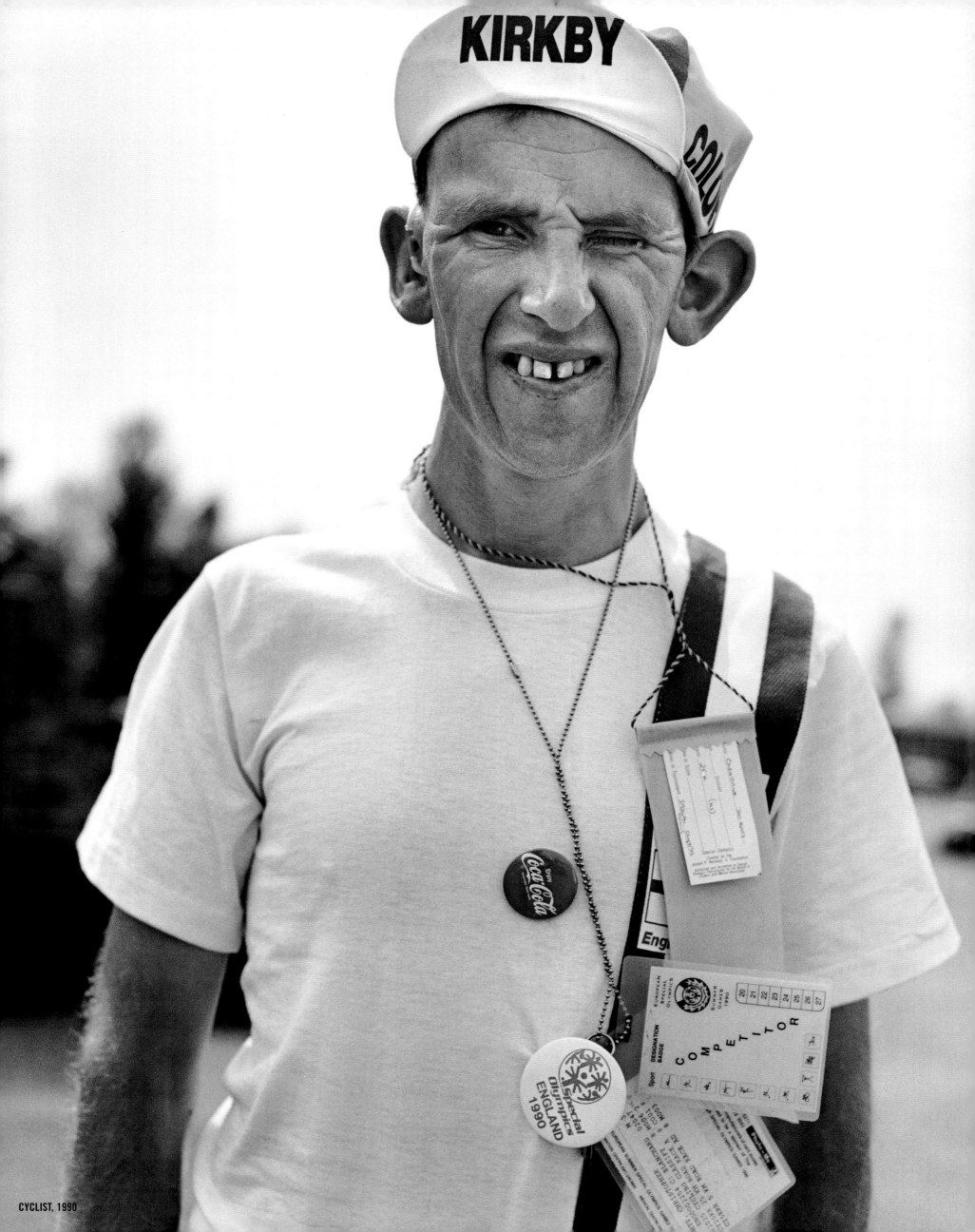

CYCLIST, 1990

GYMNAST, 1995

WHITNEY RIEPE, 1998

BOXER, 1986

BASKETBALL PLAYERS, 1985

T he glory of sport is witnessing a well-coached team perform as a single unit, striving for a common goal and ultimately bringing distinction to the jersey the players represent.

DICK VITALE

PAT RILEY, 1992

RUNNER, 1990

S

ports provides an arena to practice on yourself. I love the way playing volleyball makes me feel. I love that I can use my body to do something. No amount of money or recognition has ever brought me the same feeling of accomplishment.

GABRIELLE REECE

GABRIELLE REECE, 1994

DAN GABLE, 1998

PICABO STREET, 1996

MICHAL PESZYNKSI, 1995

AL TOON, 1988

I missed winning a medal in Seoul in 1988, and rowed two or three times a day for four more years with the single-minded purpose of holding the gold in '92. Any mention of an Olympic gold filled me with want. My heart raced, my legs drove harder.

When the day of our final race arrived in 1992, I sat on my little wooden seat and searched the horizon for the finish line, barely visible 2,000 meters away. When my partner, Stephanie, and I got there, in seven minutes or so, my decade-long life as a rower would be over, its measure taken.

Stephanie's muscular back attacked every stroke. Three-quarters of the way through, pain sunk its savage teeth into my legs and blew flames down my throat, taunting me to pull harder.

When our slender thirty-foot boat crossed the finish line, Canada was several feet ahead. The difference between second and third was a matter of inches, a photo finish between us and Germany. We floated just past the line, gasping for air and squirming with lactic acid. I leaned over the gunwale and threw up. Finally the board lit up. We were third. Bronze. Failure.

Speechless, we paddled over to the medals platform. We climbed out of the boat, stood up on the dock, and hugged each other. Then we shook hands with the Germans and the Canadians. Noticing that our time on the board was 7:08, faster than we'd ever gone before, Stephanie and I shared a moment of smiling satisfaction. But as we stood together, medals around our necks, arms full of flowers, and listened to the Canadian national anthem, I felt numb.

At dinner, our coach, Holly Hatton, stood up. I braced myself. After ten years of friendship and working together, I knew I could trust whatever she was going to say, but I expected it to hurt. As Holly spoke, I took my first tiny step out of a black-and-white world where winning is everything. "There are very few Olympic medals in the world," Holly said. "You just earned one. Its value is not measured by its color, but by the commitment that went into its pursuit." In my mind's eye, I reviewed our training for that final race. Then I envisioned the race, from start to finish. We had nothing to regret, no moment of faintheartedness or weak stroke of surrender to haunt us. Our race had not been the moment of glory we had trained for and dreamed of. But it had been our very best.

———————

ANNA SEATON HUNTINGTON

JANET EVANS, 1996

ROBERTO PRUZZO, 1984

KNIGHT SISTERS, 1995

CHARLES BARKLEY, 1992

VICTOR BATTLE, 1995

The great Russian weight lifter Yuri Vlasov called them "the white moments," those incredible epiphanies of athletic action when movement is so intense and so close to perfection that time stops, everything becomes still. For the athlete it is a kind of emotional snapshot, forever remembered. The spectator can only hope that an artist with a camera has peeled the moment off the air.

Think of Michael Jordan standing on an invisible stage three feet off the ground, his hand above the hoop. Think of Greg Louganis, a knife stabbing water. Or Billie Jean King at the net. She once described how she feels after the perfect shot: "My heart pounds, my eyes get damp, and my ears feel like they're wiggling, but it's also just totally peaceful. It's almost like having an orgasm—it's exactly like that."

What a drug it must be! No wonder the great ones hardly ever quit at the top of their games. As Bill Bradley once put it, "There are not too many aspects of life where contentment follows so quickly the exhilaration of a total coordinated effort."

Those rare moments when one fills the net, clears every hurdle, feels the club as an extension of an arm.

Get the picture?

Vlasov explained, "At the peak of tremendous and victorious effort, while the blood is still pounding in your head, all suddenly becomes quiet within you. Everything seems clearer and whiter than ever before, as if great spotlights had been turned on.

"At this moment, you have the conviction that you contain all the power in the world, that you are capable of everything, that you have wings. There is no more precious moment in life than this, "the white moment," and you will work very hard for years just to taste it again."

Or to hold the image of it in your hands and look at it so hard that you can feel it, too.

ROBERT LIPSYTE

KEN GRIFFEY, JR., 1996

GEORGE FOREMAN, 1996

DAN JANSEN, 1995

DARA TORRES, 1998

Sport is one
of society's broadest common denominators.
Sports can bring good news.
It can help lift the spiritual poverty
that hovers over so many
of our children. We, in sports, can give
them the richness of spirit
that comes with being a part of a real team,
being independent and
being able to count on a brother or a
sister at any time. It is a
powerful gift to possess, that spirit—the
antidote to the loneliness
and the feeling of being unwanted
that so many are burdened with, relief from
the weight of the world.

RICHARD LAPCHICK

SOFTBALL PLAYER, 1995

JENNY THOMPSON, 1996

I believe
in human decency and
in the fun that
comes with fair play.
But most of all, I
believe in playing with
your heart, with
every fiber in your body
—fairly, squarely,
by the rules—to win.
And I believe that
any man's finest moment,
the greatest
fulfillment of all he
 holds dear, is that moment
when he has worked
his heart out and
lies exhausted on the floor
of battle—victorious.

BELA KAROLYI

ERIC PIATKOWSKI, 1994

ENYI-ABAL KOENE, 1998

I t's really impossible for athletes to grow up. On the one hand, you're still a child, still playing a game. But on the other hand, you're a super-human hero that everyone dreams of being. No wonder we have such a hard time understanding who we are.

—————————

BILLIE JEAN KING

EXTENDER

BILLIE JEAN KING, 1997

SEAN COOPER, 1998

KYRA NICHOLS, 1996

SHAQUILLE O'NEAL, 1995

Each warrior wants to leave the mark of his will, his signature, on the important acts he touches. This is not the voice of ego but of the human spirit, rising up and declaring that it has something to contribute. In every contest, there comes a moment that separates winning from losing. The true warrior understands and seizes that moment by giving an effort so intense and so intuitive that it could only be called one from the heart.

PAT RILEY

BETTY OKINO, 1992

ITALIAN GIRL, 1986

PATRICK MELVILLE, 1994

CONTORTIONIST, 1993

Dream big and dare to fail.

I have run the Iditarod thirteen times and my last finish was at the age of eighty-four. For sixty-five years I dreamed of reaching the summit of Mount Vaughan in Antarctica and did so on my eighty-ninth birthday. Do not give credence to the words *no* or *can't*. No matter how bold, dreams can be yours.

Do not yield. Remain steadfast.

COLONEL NORMAN VAUGHAN

COLONEL NORMAN VAUGHAN, 1995

JIM COURIER, 1992

MO VAUGHN, 1995

VARSITY LACROSSE TEAM, 1998

My love affair with sports began innocently as a child. I was fascinated by how fast I could run and how far I could throw a ball. In my adult life, sports has opened doors that might otherwise have remained closed to me. It has connected me to a dynamic world where individuals from all backgrounds train, compete, win, lose, and define themselves only by the physical and mental challenges set before them every day as athletes. Sport is undeniably our society's greatest equalizer.

ROBIN ROBERTS

131

PAOLO MALDINI, 1994

KATHY "WILDCAT" COLLINS, 1998

NICOL HLINKA, 1996

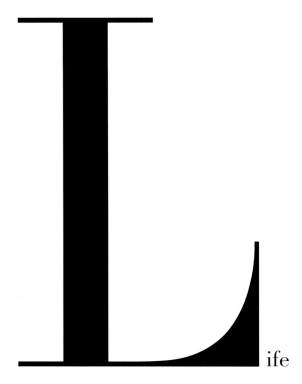

is full of defining moments—
you either define the moment or the moment
defines you.

————————

LYN ST. JAMES

LYN ST. JAMES, 1995

EQUESTRIAN, 1995

KAREEM ABDUL-JABBAR, 1991

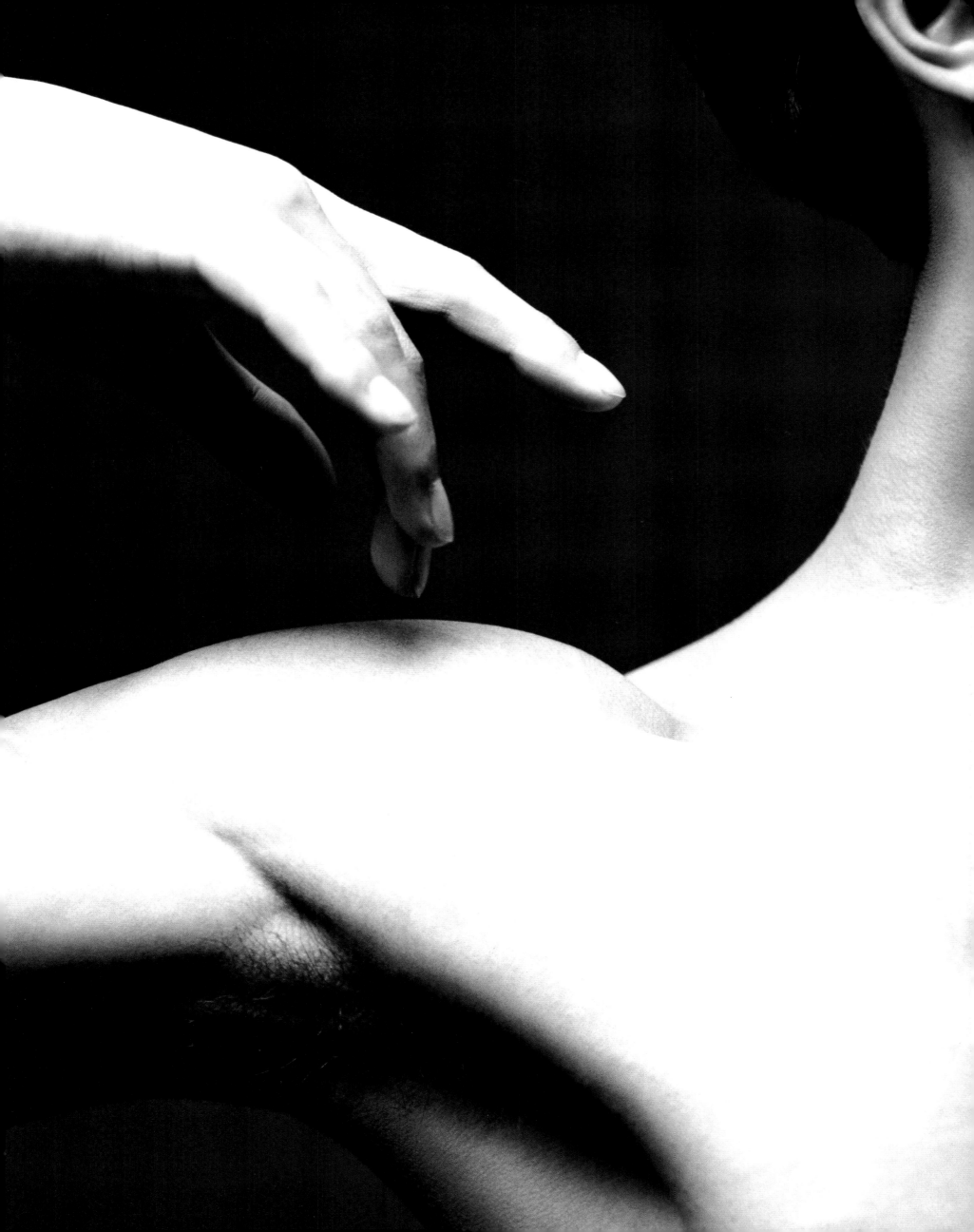

I'm not worried about anything. I'm not fearing any man. Mine eyes have seen the glory of the coming of the Lord.

—DR. MARTIN LUTHER KING

February 1962: My father and I were too nervous to sit, so we stood in the TV room of my grandmother's house on First Avenue in Phoenix, Illinois. The radio was on, tuned to the sports event of the year: brash young Cassius Marcelus Clay versus the Bear, Charles "Sonny" Liston, heavyweight champion of the world.

Clay had caused an odd transformation in the country, in our household, and within the African-American community.

Years before, outrage had been directed against Liston when he went up against Floyd Patterson, the Model Negro, the more ideal Negro. Liston, with his criminal record and mob connections, was the Thug. Civil rights leaders, even the president of the United States, rooted for Patterson, spoke of Patterson as champion, as something good for "The Race." Liston pulverized him, not once but twice—the triumph of Evil over Good. But now here was this young, brash, dashing, daring Cassius Marcelus Clay confronting an older generation—with his tongue, his taunts, and his impudence.

Later, there would be talk of Clay's connection to Black Muslims, that militant group. That separatist group. Wasn't integration what black folk wanted all along? Suddenly "Evil" became relative and

MUHAMMAD ALI, 1998

redefined. Sonny Liston became reassuring to an older generation who hoped, with more fervor than ever, that Clay would be crushed, silenced, dashed to bits by the Bear. "Enough of this militant stuff. Enough of this talk of separation, of white men as blue-eyed devils. Let us live peacefully within the illusion of our captivity." Some reveled in Clay's coming destruction.

But in 1962, as my dad and I prepared to listen to the fight, our nervousness kept building. Suddenly my father went over, grabbed his coat, and headed toward the back door.

"Where are you going?" I asked.

"In the backyard," he answered.

"Why?"

"I'm going to catch Clay!"

Thirty-six years later, "Clay" still has not landed. He beat Liston, the Thug, twice, but also humiliated the Christian Patterson, who refused to call him by his new name, Muhammad Ali.

Ali became the first universal, seemingly omnipresent black man. He did things, said things, we never imagined doing, but only dreamt of doing. Like changing his slave name from Clay to Ali, refusing to be inducted into the army, revising everything he'd worked for, including the heavyweight championship, on principle. We saw Ali stripped of his title and then whipped, like those "Bad Nigga" slaves of old. Publicly.

His courage gave many of us strength: black and white, rich and poor. For me, Ali introduced the concept of principle, which I cherish to this day. There was something greater in life than wealth, though wealth is fine and has its place. Something greater in life than fame, though fame is fine and has its place.

What there is, is Glory. A prize that comes only at the end of the day. For only the true hero can say, "I'm not worried about anything. I'm not fearing any man. Mine eyes have seen the glory of the coming of the Lord."

WILLIAM H. RHODEN

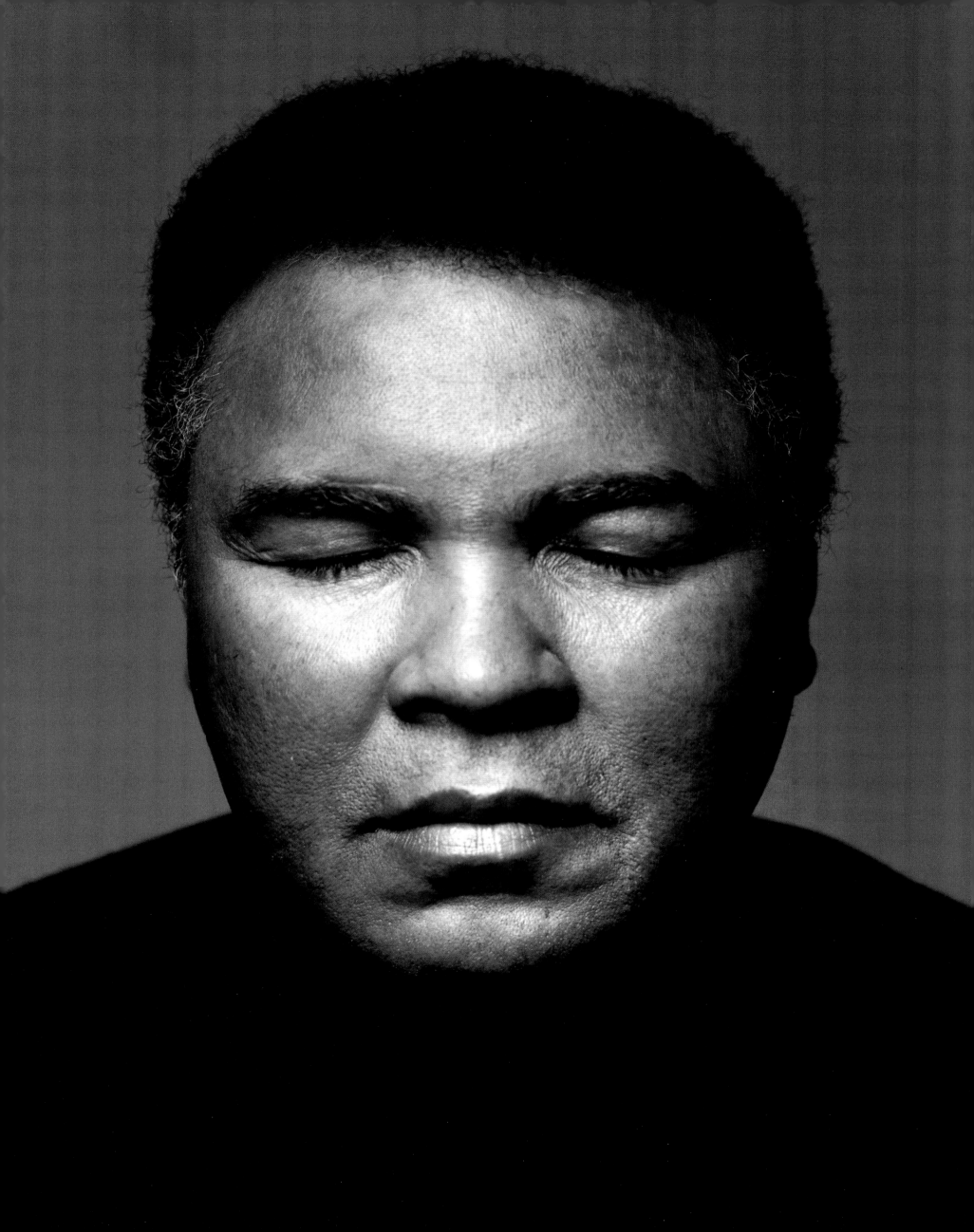

Muhammad Ali
Humanitarian

Dr. Harvey H. Corman, 1942
Lacrosse goalie: Tufts University, 1938–1942

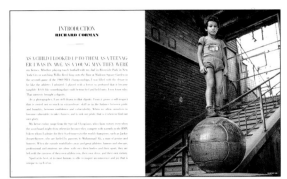

Italian boy, 1984

Peter Boal, 1995
Principal dancer: New York City Ballet

Jackie Joyner-Kersee, 1996
Track & field: founder and CEO, JJK Youth Center Foundation;
world record holder in heptathlon since 1986; Olympic gold
medalist, heptathlon (1988, 1992) and long jump (1988)

Blair Underwood, 1995
Actor: portrayed Jackie Robinson in the HBO film *Soul of the
Game* (1996)

Felix "Tito" Trinidad, 1998
Boxer: IBF welterweight champion (1993–)

Sharon Monplaisir, 1992
Fencer: Olympian (1984, 1988, 1992)

Gail Devers, 1992
Sprinter/hurdler: Olympic gold medalist, 100 meters (1992,
1996)

Lance Armstrong, 1996
Cyclist: Olympian (1992, 1996), world champion (1993),
Tour de France stage winner (1993, 1995)

Kyle Brady, 1995
Football player: New York Jets (1995–)

Allen Johnson, 1996
Hurdler: Olympic gold medalist, 110-meter hurdles (1996)

Timothy Shriver, Ph.D.
President and CEO, Special Olympics International

Special Olympian, 1990
Swimmer

Michael Jordan, 1991
Basketball player: Chicago Bulls (1984–1998; NBA
champions, 1991–1993, 1996–1998); NBA Most Valuable
Player in 1988, 1991, 1992, 1996, and 1998; Olympic team
gold medalist (1984, 1992)
Roy Firestone
Broadcaster, ESPN

Keith Van Horn, 1998
Basketball player: New Jersey Nets (1995–)

Darci Kistler, 1995
Principal dancer: New York City Ballet

Dr. Carole A. Oglesby
Sports psychologist: member of U.S. Olympic Committee and
Sports Psychology Registry

Darryl Strawberry, 1985
Baseball player: New York Yankees (1995–1998), San Francisco
Giants (1994), Los Angeles Dodgers (1990–1993), New York
Mets (1983–1989), 1983 National League Rookie of the Year

Bonnie Blair, 1998
Speed skater: Olympic gold medalist, 500 meters (1988, 1992,
1994) and 1000 meters (1988, 1992)

P.L.A.Y. Basketball Camp, 1995

Sheryl Swoopes, 1996
Basketball player: Houston Comets (1997–), Olympic team gold
medalist (1996), 1993 NCAA Player of the Year

Andres Espinosa, 1994
Marathon runner: New York City Marathon champion (1993)

Cal Ripken, Jr., 1996
Baseball player: Baltimore Orioles (1982–), record holder for
most consecutive games played at 2,131, American League
Most Valuable Player (1983), Rookie of the Year (1982)

John Starks, 1993
Basketball player: New York Knicks (1988–)

Reggie Brown, 1998
Football player: Detroit Lions (1996–1997)

Edwin Moses, 1988
Hurdler: Olympic gold medalist, 400-meter hurdles (1976,
1984)

Danny Dromgool, 1995
Soccer player: Special Olympics

Mark McCormack
Chairman and CEO, International Management Group

Michael Johnson, 1996
Track & field: Olympic gold medalist (1996); first man ever to
win the Olympic 200/400 double

Victor Battle, 1997
Basketball player: Stockton College (1988–1992)

Gail Devers, 1992
Sprinter/hurdler: Olympic gold medalist, 100 meters (1992,
1996)

John Khalie, 1995
Track & field: Special Olympics

Mariama Kpaka, 1995
Track & field: Special Olympics

Jackie Joyner-Kersee, 1992
Track & field: founder and CEO, JJK Youth Center Foundation;
world record holder in heptathlon since 1986; Olympic gold
medalist, heptathlon (1988, 1992) and long jump (1988)

Brad Hunt, 1998
Sport fisherman: Florida State Salt Water Angler champion (1992)

Aimee Mullins, 1998

Aimee Mullins, 1998
Track & field: USA Track & Field Disabled Female Athlete of the Year (1997); world record, 100- and 200-meter dash and long jump (1996); only double below-the-knee amputee to compete on an NCAA Division I track team (Georgetown University, 1996); Paralympian (1996)

Robert De Niro
Actor: Academy Award winner, *The Godfather Part II* (1974), *Raging Bull* (1980)

Roy Jones, Jr., 1995
Boxer: WBA light heavyweight champion (1998), WBC light heavyweight champion (1997), IBF super middleweight champion (1994), IBF middleweight champion (1993)

Mark Sanabria, 1996
In-line skater

Tony Tucker, 1989
Boxer: NABF heavyweight champion (1996), IBF heavyweight champion (1987)

Kim Batten, 1996
Hurdler: Olympic silver medalist, 400-meter hurdles (1996)

Maya Labat and L. B. Tejada, 1996
BMX Bikers

Rickey Jackson, 1991
Football player: San Francisco 49ers (1994–1995; Super Bowl champions, 1994); New Orleans Saints (1981–1994); six-time Pro-Bowl selection (1983–1986, 1992, 1993)

Deanna McBrearty, 1996
Dancer: corps de ballet, New York City Ballet

Jerry Rice
Football player: San Francisco 49ers (1985–), ten-time All-Pro (1986–1990, 1992–1996), NFL Player of the Year in 1987 and 1990, NFL all-time leader in touchdowns, receptions, and yards

Harry Carson, 1988
Football player: New York Giants (1976–1988; Super Bowl champions, 1982)

Nancy Kerrigan, 1992
Figure skater: Olympic silver medalist (1994), Olympic bronze medalist (1992), 1993 U.S. women's champion

Special Olympian, 1991
Track & field

Ahmad Rashad
Host, analyst, commentator, reporter and managing editor for NBC Sports

Mark O'Meara, 1998
Golfer: 1998 Masters and British Open champion; sixteen total PGA Tour victories

Tiger Woods, 1998
Golfer: 1997 Masters champion (youngest Masters champion ever, at twenty-one); six total PGA Tour victories

Luke Wilson, 1983
Actor

Owen Wilson, 1983
Actor, writer, producer

New York Yankees, 1998
Chuck Knoblauch, Derek Jeter, Paul O'Neill, Tino Martinez, Bernie Williams: 1998 World Series champions

Donna A. Lopiano, Ph.D. Executive director, Women's Sports Foundation

Antonio Cabrini, 1984
Soccer player: Italian World Cup team member, 1982

Julie Kent, 1992
Principal dancer: American Ballet Theatre

Connie Price-Smith, 1988
Shot-putter and discus thrower: ranked #1 U.S. shot-putter in
1988, 1990, 1993–1995 and #1 U.S. discus thrower in 1990,
1993, and 1994

Bud Greenspan
Writer, producer, director; president, Cappy Productions, Inc.

Special Olympian, 1990
Cyclist

Special Olympian, 1995
Gymnast

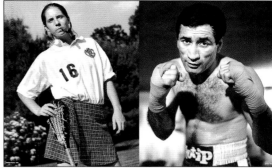

Whitney Riepe, 1998
Varsity lacrosse player: Miss Porter's School

Argentinean boxer, 1986

Special Olympians, 1995
Basketball players

Dick Vitale
Basketball commentator, ESPN/ABC

Pat Riley, 1992
President and head coach: Miami Heat (1995–)

Special Olympian, 1990
Runner

Gabrielle Reece, 1994
Volleyball player: 1997 WBVL; member of league
co-championship team Nike; WBVL Kills leader
(1993–1996); WBVL Offensive Player of the Year
(1994–1995); WBVL kills and blocks leader (1993)

Dan Gable, 1998
Wrestler: University of Iowa head wrestling coach (1977–1997),
with fifteen NCAA team trophies; Olympic gold medalist (1972);
gold medalist, world championships (1971)

Picabo Street, 1996
Downhill skier: Olympic gold medalist (1998), silver medalist
(1994)

Michal Peszynksi, 1995
Equestrian: Special Olympics

Al Toon, 1988
Football player: New York Jets (1985–1992); Pro-Bowl
(1986–1988)

Anna Seaton Huntington
Rower: Olympic bronze medalist (1992)

Janet Evans, 1996
Swimmer: Olympic gold medalist, 400-meter freestyle (1988),
400-meter individual medley (1988), 800-meter freestyle
(1988, 1992)

Roberto Pruzzo, 1984
Soccer player: Italian championship team member, Rome
(1983)

Knight Sisters, 1995
Track & field: Special Olympics

Charles Barkley, 1992
Basketball player: Houston Rockets (1996–), Phoenix Suns
(1992–1996), Philadelphia 76ers (1984–1992), Olympic team
gold medalist (1992, 1996), NBA All-Star (1986–1996), NBA
Most Valuable Player of 1993

Victor Battle, 1995
Basketball player: Stockton College (1988–1992)

Robert Lipsyte
Columnist, *The New York Times*; author of eighteen books,
including *Sportsworld: An American Dreamland* and *Free to Be
Muhammad Ali*

Ken Griffey, Jr., 1996
Baseball player: Seattle Mariners (1989–), Gold Glove Award (1990–1998), American League Most Valuable Player of 1997; 1994 American League home run champion, Most Valuable Player in 1992 All-Star Game

George Foreman, 1996
Boxer: world heavyweight champion (1973–1974, 1994–1995, 1995–1996), Olympic gold medalist (1968)

Dan Jansen, 1995
Speed skater: Olympic gold medalist, 500 meters (1994)

Dara Torres, 1998
Swimmer: 1992 U.S. national team captain; Olympic gold medalist, 400-meter freestyle relay (1984)

Richard Lapchick
Director, Center for the Study of Sport in Society, Northeastern University; author of nine books, including *Sport in Society: Equal Opportunity or Business as Usual*

Special Olympian, 1995
Softball player

Malik Sealy, 1989
Basketball player: Detroit Pistons (1997–)

Jenny Thompson, 1996
Swimmer: Olympic gold medalist, 400-meter freestyle relay (1992, 1996), 800-meter freestyle relay (1996), 400-meter medley (1992)

Bela Karolyi
Gymnastics: head coach of U.S. Olympic team (1988, 1992), head coach of Rumanian Olympic team (1976, 1980)

Eric Piatkowski, 1994
Basketball player: Los Angeles Clippers (1995–)

Marcus Schaffer, 1996
Skateboarder

Enyi-Abal Koene, 1998
Varsity crew member: Miss Porter's School

Billie Jean King, 1997
Tennis player: co-founder and director, World Team Tennis, Inc.; twenty Wimbledon titles

Sean Cooper, 1998
New York City bike messenger

Kyra Nichols, 1996
Principal dancer: New York City Ballet

Skateboarder and in-line skater, 1996

Shaquille O'Neal, 1995
Basketball player: Los Angeles Lakers (1996–), Orlando Magic (1992–1996), Olympic team gold medalist (1996), NBA All-Star (1992–1997)

Herbert John Perez, 1992
Tae Kwan Do world champion, Olympic gold medalist (1992)

Pat Riley, 1992
President and head coach: Miami Heat (1995–)

Betty Okino, 1992
Gymnast: Olympic team bronze medalist (1992)

Italian girl, 1986

Patrick Melville, 1994
Former boxer

Contortionist, 1993
Ringling Brothers Barnum & Bailey Circus

Colonel Norman Vaughan, 1995
Explorer; team member on Admiral Byrd's 1929 expedition to
the South Pole; thirteen-time Iditarod sled-dog race competitor

Jim Courier, 1992
Tennis player: Australian Open champion (1992, 1993), French
Open champion (1991, 1992)

Mo Vaughn, 1995
Baseball player: Boston Red Sox (1991–), American League
Most Valuable Player of 1995

Miss Porter's School Varsity lacrosse team, 1998

Robin Roberts
Sports anchor, ESPN/ABC

Paolo Maldini, 1994
Soccer player: Italian World Cup team captain (1994, 1998)

Kathy "Wildcat" Collins, 1998
Boxer: IFBA women's world welterweight champion (1997)

Jim Carey, 1995
Hockey player: Boston Bruins (1997–), Washington Capitols
(1994–1997)

Nicol Hlinka, 1996
Principal dancer: New York City Ballet

Lyn St. James, 1998
Race-car driver: Indianapolis 500 competitor (1993–1995),
1992 Rookie of the Year

Special Olympian, 1995
Equestrian

Kareem Abdul-Jabbar, 1991
Basketball player: Los Angeles Lakers (1975–1989); NBA
champions 1980, 1982, 1985, 1987, 1988), Milwaukee Bucks
(1969–1975; NBA champions, 1971); NBA Most Valuable
Player in 1971, 1972, 1974, 1976, 1977, and 1980

Edward Liang, 1996
Dancer: soloist, New York City Ballet

William H. Rhoden
Sports columnist, *The New York Times*; author of *Lost Tribe,
Wandering: The Dilemma of Black Athletes in America*

Muhammad Ali, 1998
Humanitarian

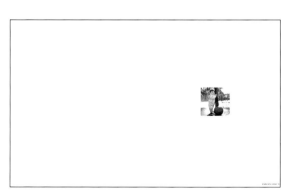

William Harvey Corman, 1998

Chris Kotes, 1993
Former NCAA baseball player

I want
to express my deepest gratitude to the
contributors and athletes who appear in this book.
Their time, energy, words, and eyes have made *Glory*
a dream come true for me.

I am most thankful to my wife, Patricia, for coordinating
this project with such skill, perseverance, and grace.
Without her love and support, *Glory* just would not be *Glory*.

Thanks to Doris Cooper for her intelligence, enthusiasm
and spirited encouragement, which inspired me daily.

Thanks to Michael Murphy for believing so strongly in this
project and for being such a sports aficionado.

I owe a debt of gratitude to my dear friend
Yolanda Cuomo for her brilliance and wonderful
sense of humor. Tanti bacioni.

Thanks to Paul Chan for his technical expertise
and years of assistance, which are greatly appreciated.

Thanks to Peter Chin for his serenity and steadfast assistance.

Thanks to Eric Rasmussen for his Light.

Many thanks to John Delaney and David Frawley
for their masterful and exquisite prints.

Thanks to Jenny Scheffer Stevens, who has the heart
of an angel and has brought so much warmth
and hard work to this project.

Thanks to Wanda Luz Octaviano for her optimism
and unrelenting ability to make things happen, however
improbable or impossible the task.

Thanks to Alexis Brentani Ritter for keeping the tradition alive.

Thanks to Chris Bishop for his beautiful work.

A warm thanks to Cohl Katz and Lori Madugno-Alpert
for their unfailing support and friendship, which goes
well beyond the call of duty.

Thanks to Frances Spivey, my devoted studio manager,
for holding everything together in spite of me.

Thanks to Stockland Martel Agency for enabling
me to photograph some of my heroes.

Thanks to Kristi Novagaard for her diligence and precision.

Thanks to Paul Fedorko for giving *Glory* a home.

Thanks to Tom Nau for his calm and support.

A very special thank you to Ruedi Hofmann for being
there twenty-four hours a day, 365 days a year.

Thanks to Dick Avedon for his eternal inspiration.

Thank you to my mom, Cis Corman, for her remarkable strength.

Dear William, my son, you will always be my Glory.

Library of Congress Cataloging-in-Publication Data

Corman, Richard.
Glory ; photographs of athletes / Richard Corman. — 1st ed.
p.   cm.
Includes index.
ISBN 0-688-15898-6
1. Sports. 2. Sports—Pictorial works. 3. Athletes. 4. Athletes—Pictorial works.
5. Photography of sports. I. Title. II. Title: Photographs of athletes.
GV704.C67   1999
796—dc21   98-54381
CIP
Printed in Hong Kong
First Edition

1 2 3 4 5 6 7 8 9 10

BOOK DESIGN BY YOLANDA CUOMO, NYC
Design associate: Kristi Novagaard
Gallery representation by SoHo Triad Fine Arts, New York, New York

www.williammorrow.com